GREEN-COLLAR CAREERS

LEARNING GREEN

CAREERS IN EDUCATION

By Suzy Gazlay

CRABTREE
Publishing Company
www.crabtreebooks.com

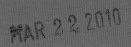

Crabtree Publishing Company

Author: Suzy Gazlay
Publishing plan research and development:
 Sean Charlebois, Reagan Miller
 Crabtree Publishing Company
Editors: Mark Sachner, Molly Aloian
Proofreader: Reagan Miller
Editorial director: Kathy Middleton
Photo research: Ruth Owen
Designer: Westgrapix/Tammy West
Production coordinator: Margaret Amy Salter
Prepress technician: Katherine Berti
Production: Kim Richardson
Curriculum adviser: Suzy Gazlay, M.A.
Editorial consultant: James Marten, Ph.D.; Chair, Department
 of History, Marquette University, Milwaukee, Wisconsin

Written, developed, and produced by Water Buffalo Books

Photographs and reproductions
Alamy: Tom Gardner: page 11 (bottom); Jiri Rezac: page 40 (left)
Corbis: Connie Rica: page 6 (left); Jonathan Blair: page 37 (top);
 Bettmann: page 38 (bottom)
FLPA: Tim Fitzharris: page 8 (bottom); Paul Hobson: page 11 (right);
 L Lee Rue: page 34 (top); STELLA: page 39 (right)
Gettyimages: MPI: page 16 (left); Tod Korol: page 36 (bottom)
John Muir's Birthplace: page 13 (right)
High Sierra Volunteer Trail Crew: page 33 (left)
Holt-Atherton Special Collections, University of the Pacific Library. John
 Muir Papers. Copyright 1984 Muir-Hanna Trust: MuirFiche2Frame0080:
 page 5 (right); f24-1305: page 7 (bottom left); f23-1252: page 12 (bottom);
 MuirFiche4Frame0184: page 17 (bottom right); f23-1247: page 18 (left);
 MuirReel23Journal01P088-089: page 25 (bottom); Shone1.3.1.2: page 25
 (right); f24-1349: page 27 (bottom); MSS305.1.3.3.1.4: page 28 (top);
 Shone1.3.1.6: page 30 (top); MuirFiche5Frame0282: page 30 (bottom);
 f25-1379: page 31 (bottom) Courtesy of the Library of Congress: Image
 3b00011u: front cover (inset); Image 3b00011u: page 1; Image 3g04698u:
 page 5 (bottom left); Image 3b43690u: page 7 (right); Image 3b00011u:
 page 8 (top left); Image 6a19572u: page 32 (top); Image 3b00011u: back cover
Courtesy National Park Service, Museum Management Program and John
 Muir National Historic Site, California: Commemorative Envelope "John
 Muir: American Naturalist" with Stamp: JOMU 4261 B: page 41 (top right)
Alastair Seagrott: page 9 (left)
Shutterstock: front cover main; page 4 (left); page 10 (left); page 14 (top left);
 page 14 (top center left); page 14 (top center right); page 14 (top right);
 page 14 (bottom left); page 14 (bottom center left); page 14 (bottom center
 right); page 14 (bottom right); page 15 (right center); page 15 (right bottom);
 page 17 (top left); page 20 (left); page 22 (top); page 22 (bottom); page 23
 (right); page 23 (bottom); page 24 (left); page 26 (left); page 27 (right); page
 28 (bottom); page 31 (top); page 32 (bottom); page 34 (top right); page 35
 (bottom); page 35 (right); page 39 (bottom); page 42 (bottom)
Sierra Club: map of 1,000 mile walk: page 21 (top right)
Superstock: page 13 (bottom); page 21 (bottom)
United States Mint Image: page 41 (center right)
Wikipedia Creative Commons Attribution ShareAlike 2.5 licence:
 page 42 (top)
Wisconsin Historical Society: WHi-40625: page 17 (top right); WHi-10983:
 page 19 (right)

Library and Archives Canada Cataloguing in Publication

 Available at Library and Archives Canada

Library of Congress Cataloging-in-Publication Data

Gazlay, Suzy.
 Learning green : careers in education / Suzy Gazlay.
  p. cm. -- (Green-collar careers)

 Includes index.

 ISBN 978-0-7787-4865-6 (pbk. : alk. paper) -- ISBN 978-0-7787-4854-0
(reinforced library binding : alk. paper)
 1. Environmental education--Vocational guidance. 2. Teaching--
Vocational guidance. I. Title. II. Series.

 GE60.G39 2010
 333.72071--dc22

 2009028074

Crabtree Publishing Company
www.crabtreebooks.com   1-800-387-7650

**Published
in Canada**
Crabtree Publishing
616 Welland Ave.
St. Catharines, Ontario
L2M 5V6

**Published in
the United States**
Crabtree Publishing
PMB16A
350 Fifth Ave., Suite 3308
New York, NY 10118

**Published in the
United Kingdom**
Crabtree Publishing
Maritime House
Basin Road North, Hove
BN41 1WR

**Published
in Australia**
Crabtree Publishing
386 Mt. Alexander Rd.
Ascot Vale (Melbourne)
VIC 3032

CONTENTS

What is important to you about protecting the environment? Are you concerned about climate change? Do you sometimes wonder how you can figure out your family's carbon footprint? Do you recycle at school or at home? Can you name an alternative energy source? Are these questions important to you? Two generations ago, most students your age probably wouldn't have known what most of these things meant!

Even in your parents' generation, there was a gap between what scientists knew about the environment and what the general public knew. Today, issues such as the need to save energy or reduce pollution are hot topics. That's a very good thing, because our planet is in trouble!

How did you first become aware of green issues? Was it in the classroom, going online, watching a TV show, or reading a book? Today, most young people know that wind or solar power is greener than electricity produced by burning coal. They routinely recycle, and they know that this is the best way to save energy and resources.

Below: A power plant burning coal to produce electricity. In the United States, 90 percent of the coal that is mined is used to produce electricity. The problem with this means of generating electricity is that it produces carbon emissions that are causing climate change.

CAREER PROFILE

LIVE LEARNING IN THE CLASSROOM: TEACHING BIOLOGY AND ENVIRONMENTAL SCIENCES

I have always loved animal life—from tiny to huge. Over the years I have maintained many different kinds of animals as pets and companions. I keep animals in my classroom so my students can learn about the incredible diversity of life on Earth. They can see living creatures right there in front of them and not simply as pictures in a book or on the Web. Among the animals in my classroom were a variety of insects from hissing roaches to dragonflies collected as nymphs and allowed to emerge as adults; spiders, crayfish, snails, earthworms, frogs, lizards, turtles, pheasants, and a chinchilla, my all-time favorite classroom pet. We watch live animals move, breathe, eat, sleep, and give birth. All the while, my students learn to care for and respect these animals.

Teaching people about the wonderful living things that are here on Earth is important if we want them to know these organisms and appreciate them. Ultimately, it will be only the people who know about them who will be the ones who will help conserve the lands and waters in which those organisms live—and even preserve their lives.

Kirk Janowiak
Secondary School Instructor of Biology and Environmental Sciences
Delhi Community High School
Delhi, Indiana

HOW THE WORLD LEARNED ABOUT CLIMATE CHANGE

Scientists have been recording and studying climate change for nearly 200 years. In 1827, a French scientist, Jean-Baptiste Joseph Fourier, suggested that the atmosphere was acting like a greenhouse in warming the Earth. It took 112 years for the term "greenhouse effect" to come into common use enough to be included in the dictionary.

In the 1950s, scientists proved the connection between increased levels of carbon dioxide and rising temperatures in the atmosphere. The term "global warming" gradually became more familiar. In 1969, it was added to the dictionary. In 1979, the first World Climate Conference identified climate change as a major concern. In 1988, global warming made headlines around the world when scientists blamed it for a major drought in the United States.

According to a national poll taken in 1992, 22 percent of Americans said they didn't understand anything at all about global warming. In 2004, a similar poll showed that only 6 percent didn't understand what global warming meant. Today, it's hard to read a newspaper, in print or online, without coming across breaking news about climate change or some sort of environmental concern. Each step along the way has been the result of teaching and learning green.

Earth in Danger

The burning of fossil fuels, such as coal to make electricity and oil to power our cars, is causing climate change—Earth is getting warmer. We are using up the planet's store of non-renewable resources such as oil and coal. The chemicals we spray onto our crops to make them grow faster or to protect them from pests and disease are polluting rivers and killing wildlife. Wild habitats, and the animals that live in them, are being destroyed to make space for towns or farmland.

U.S. president Ronald Reagan stands in a drought-stricken cornfield in 1988. With him are farmers showing him the stunted growth of their crops. Today, we know that rising global temperatures, due to climate change, will cause parts of the world to become too dry for food to grow. Our weather will also become more extreme with hurricanes, heat waves, and torrential rain.

Your Green Generation

When your grandparents were students, these environmental issues may not have been talked about in school that much. People weren't as concerned about switching off the lights when they left the room or throwing an empty can into the general trash.

On the other hand, you probably already know quite a bit about "green" issues. You likely know that turning off a light will save energy and cut down on the amount of oil or coal that needs to be burned. You may know that making a new can from a recycled one uses less energy than starting with new metal.

Protestors at a rally in New York campaign for an 80 percent cut in carbon emissions worldwide by 2050. The environmental movement has a long history of raising awareness through marches and rallies.

THE FATHER OF ENVIRONMENTALISM

In 1845, U.S. author Henry David Thoreau built a small, rough house by Walden Pond near Concord, Massachusetts. He lived there for two years, studying nature and writing. He believed that people should live simply and be aware of both their own nature and that of the natural world around them.

After Thoreau moved back to Concord, he continued to write essays and books. His journals were filled with detailed notes about his walks in the woods, as well as his hiking travels in other wild areas. He wrote with passion, blending scientific knowledge with appreciation for all that nature contributes to our lives. He was one of the first to write of the need to protect and preserve wild areas.

Thoreau wanted people to see and value the natural world as he did. Even so, he might be surprised to know that, more than 160 years later, many people consider his essays and books to be the beginning of environmentalism!

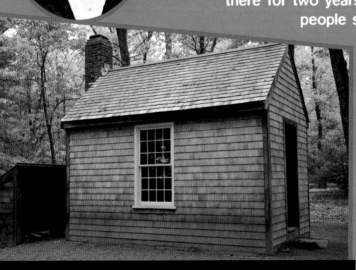

At the Walden Pond State Reservation, guests can visit this replica of Henry David Thoreau's woodland house. Thoreau understood that watching nature close up—a bird feeding her young or the leaves of a tree changing color in the fall—gives us a deep appreciation of the environment.

WAKE-UP CALL

American writer Henry David Thoreau may have laid the foundation for environmentalism, but it was a quiet, shy biologist and writer who triggered the environmental movement. In 1962, Rachel Carson (shown here with a group of kids on a nature outing) published the book *Silent Spring*. In it, she described the effects of herbicides and pesticides on birds and other living beings, including humans. These chemicals sprayed on plants and the soil did more than kill harmful insects and weeds, she said. The animals that ate the sprayed plants took in the poison, too. If they survived, the chemicals, especially DDT, stayed in their body tissue forever. Thus DDT was passed right along the food chain.

"Can anyone believe it is possible to lay down such a barrage of poisons on the surface of the earth without making it unfit for all life?" Carson asked. "They should not be called 'insecticides' but 'biocides.'"

The chemical companies immediately fought back. They argued that without pesticides, insects would destroy the crops—but Carson had already gotten the public's attention. The discussion became a national debate, with the public mostly siding with Carson.

Through her research and writing, this one courageous biologist educated both the public and the lawmakers. The widespread use of pesticides was restricted, and DDT was banned completely. People began paying closer attention to environmental issues.

"If a child is to keep alive his inborn sense of wonder . . . he needs the companionship of at least one adult who can share it, rediscovering with him the joy, excitement and mystery of the world we live in. . . . I sincerely believe that for the child, and for the parent seeking to guide him, it is not half so important to know as to feel. If facts are the seeds that later produce knowledge and wisdom, then the emotions and the impressions of the senses are the fertile soil in which the seeds must grow. The years of early childhood are the time to prepare the soil."

Rachel Carson, *The Sense of Wonder*, 1956

Do you remember when you first learned these things? Maybe it was during a science lesson in school. Perhaps you watched a TV documentary or read about saving the planet online or in a magazine.

Teaching and Learning Green

Today, there are a lot of ways in which people can "learn green." They can find out why they should be concerned about some of the things that are happening to our planet and how to stop these things from taking place. The information is starting to get out there, but more could be done.

There are still many people around the world who just don't know much about the environment. Many people don't understand the importance of living and thinking green—or they may be misinformed. This is why learning green is so important for people of all ages.

Below: Scientists watch as a glacier in Alaska calves—melts and breaks up. Events such as this are a serious reminder of the effects of global warming on our planet's polar regions.

Below, right: Davis Guggenheim (left) and Al Gore are shown with the 2007 Academy Award for Best Documentary Feature won by *An Inconvenient Truth*.

AN INCONVENIENT TRUTH— LEARNING THROUGH FILM AND BOOKS

It's unusual for environmental science to make it onto the big screen, but in 2006, *An Inconvenient Truth*, a documentary film about climate change, became a box office sensation. The film was directed by Davis Guggenheim and presented by former United States vice president Al Gore. *An Inconvenient Truth* grossed millions at the box office and won two Academy Awards. More importantly, using the medium of film brought the issue of climate change to the notice of millions of people who had not previously taken an interest in the subject.

Al Gore published a book, also named *An Inconvenient Truth*, which served as a companion to the movie. The book uses scientific data in text and images to show how climate change is occurring around the world. Satellite images show that the polar ice caps and glaciers in Greenland and Antarctica are melting due to the higher temperatures brought about by global warming. This will cause sea levels to rise. Dramatic, computer-drawn maps show how low-lying areas around the world will be flooded if sea levels continue to rise.

9

Right now, our planet's future is on the line. If we are going to stop climate change and protect the Earth, we will need even more educators teaching green and spreading the word about how we must care for our planet. Those educators might be scientists or teachers. They might be activists or writers. They may even be bloggers, songwriters, or filmmakers. One thing is for sure: Their work will be crucial to all our futures. Maybe YOU could be one of them!

Me, a Teacher?

A great thing about learning is that it goes both ways. A person who knows about something can teach others about it, too. We teach and learn from each other all the time! Think about that day you helped someone with a tricky math problem. Maybe you've shown a younger child how to ride a bike. Perhaps you've popped up with the answer to a question when everybody else was stumped. If you've done any of these things, you've been helping others learn—that is, you've been teaching.

Wildlife filmmakers and photographers can have a huge impact on millions of people through their work. Here, a photographer takes photos of an Emperor penguin family in Antarctica. Emperor penguins are just one of the many species of animals that will be in danger if climate change continues to melt polar ice.

Teaching isn't just about knowing the facts. The best teachers can bring a subject alive and inspire their students to want to find out more—in class and outside of school. Could you take your passion for the environment and inspire others to become conservationists?

Could songwriting be the way that you pass on the green message? From Joni Mitchell's "Big Yellow Taxi" (1970), in which Mitchell sings of the destruction of a natural paradise to make room for a parking lot; to Marvin Gaye's "Mercy Mercy Me (The Ecology)" (1971), which bemoans the pollution that is poisoning our planet; to Miley Cyrus's "Wake Up America" (2008) call to action, musicians and songwriters have always used songs as a way to raise environmental awareness.

UNDERWATER CONVERSATIONS: MARINE MAMMAL RESEARCH SCIENTIST

Marine mammals, such as whales and dolphins, live in a world where vision is extremely limited. They rely primarily on sound—listening and echolocation—to get information about their environment. Echolocation is the ability to locate objects by sending out sounds that are reflected back. The animals communicate with each other through vocal sounds.

One goal of my research is to show the importance of the underwater environment as a communication channel for marine mammals. Human activities such as shipping, drilling, and military sonar (on submarines, for example) are turning the seas into an increasingly noisy place. Most of us humans keep our ears above the surface, so we aren't aware of the effects of our acoustic (noise) pollution. Technology exists that could reduce the impact of our noise upon marine mammals.

Most of this technology is not being used. It is my hope that my studies will prove that marine mammals use acoustic communication to get food, find mates, and stay in contact with group members. If my research can show that this communication is an essential life process and not just "chatter," I will be a happy man.

Dr. Volker Deecke
Research Scientist
Sea Mammal Research Unit
Scottish Oceans Institute
University of St. Andrews
Fife, Scotland

Have you ever thought about teaching as a career? Can you picture yourself standing in front of a classroom? That's one possibility, but there are plenty of others. You could teach kids, adults, or community groups. You could teach in a classroom or outside in a national park or in a zoo. Many interesting and exciting opportunities await those who want to teach "green."

Oh, no, not in front of a group...

If standing in front of a group of people sounds a little scary to you, don't worry. It's far from being your only option. There are plenty of other ways—great ways—to help people learn.

The Cool Seas Roadshow (shown above left and right) is a fantastic way to teach young children about the need to protect endangered marine animals. Imagine being just five years old and having the chance to come face to face with a life-size shark or orca!

An orca breaches (launches) itself from the sea. The work of research scientists such as Dr. Volker Deecke helps the scientific community understand more about wild animals. In turn, this information can be passed onto the general public.

THE COOL SEAS ROADSHOW

The Marine Conservation Society (MCS) is a UK-based charity that raises awareness of the need to care for our oceans and marine life. The MCS campaigns to set up "Marine Protected Areas" or MPAs—areas of sea that have special protection. Inside an MPA, activities such as commercial fishing or drilling for oil and gas are banned or closely monitored. This allows plants and animals within the area to flourish and gives threatened species the chance to increase their numbers. The MCS also campaigns to clean up pollution such as sewage, industrial chemicals, and litter. They work to influence the government to put in place strict laws for dumping waste into the ocean, and they arrange beach clean-ups.

One important aspect of the MCS's work is education. Their campaigns help educate people of all ages about marine conservation. The Cool Seas Roadshow takes the MCS's message directly into schools. The show uses life-size inflatable models of such animals as whales, dolphins, sharks, seals, and turtles to teach children about marine life.

Do you like to write or blog? Are you interested in writing books, articles, or newsletters? How about stories or songs? These are also effective ways to teach.

It doesn't stop there. People learn from photographs and art, movies and television programs. Environmental organizations have the huge challenge of informing the public, often through the materials they produce in print and online. People who design, create, and keep the information up to date are part of the team. It's a multimedia world, with any number of ways to get the word out—and new technology is being developed all the time!

Scientists as Educators

Every day, all around the world, scientists are discovering more about the natural world. They begin with what others have learned and build upon it. As they carry out their research and investigations, scientists report about what they have found and what it means.

Above: At the Millennium Seed Bank in the United Kingdom, an international effort is underway to safeguard seeds from flowering plants that are threatened. The scientists have a goal—to collect and protect over 24,000 species of seeds by 2010.

Every plant, whether it is a giant sequioa tree, a garden rose, or a desert cactus (shown here) has its own important place in an ecosystem. Like wild animals, plants are essential for life on Earth and need to be protected. Scientists estimate that up to 100,000 plant species are currently in danger of extinction. It's important that people are educated about the importance of plant life to our planet's future.

CAREER PROFILE

IN THE PLANT MUSEUM: IDENTIFYING PLANTS

I work in a herbarium as part of the Cooperative Extension Service at a state university. A herbarium is like a museum for plants. Specimens are collected, identified, dried, preserved for study, and organized in a system much as you'd find in a library. The extension service is sponsored by the Department of Agriculture to provide information to the public.

My particular work is identifying plants that people send or bring in and answering questions about them. I use a microscope and reference books, and of course I can refer to plant specimens in the herbarium collection.

On a typical day, I open "plant mail" and sort and record specimens that have been sent in. I identify the plants and prepare replies to questions. Sometimes people call with questions, so I deal with those. I especially enjoy it when individuals come in and I am able to work with them directly. I don't do much work outside, but at times it's possible that I'll visit a location where a plant is growing.

The best part of my job is being able to share plant information with the public. People who contact me need help with plant information for various reasons. I have many stories about unusual reasons that plants were sent to me for identification. Perhaps the most memorable is the specimen that was sent in by the police in relation to a human death.

Iralee Barnard
Herbarium Extension Assistant
Kansas State University Cooperative
Extension Service
Manhattan, Kansas

ONE BILLION TREES

Sometimes all it takes is one exciting idea to educate millions of people about an issue. Worldwide, trees are being cut down to make space for farmland or development. Trees are vital to life on Earth. They produce much of the oxygen we breathe. They absorb carbon dioxide (which is a greenhouse gas) from the atmosphere and store it. They are food for some animals and the habitat of millions of birds, insects, and other animals. Saving trees is a vital part of saving our planet.

In 2004, Professor Wangari Maathai of Kenya launched a campaign called Plant for the Planet: Billion Tree Campaign. Professor Maathai had already founded Kenya's Green Belt Movement, a campaign that has planted 30 million trees in 12 African countries. In 2004, Professor Maathai decided to take her idea to the world!

Since then, the campaign has grown. Under the management of UNEP (United Nations Environment Program), the campaign is now working to plant seven billion trees. Private individuals, schools, companies, cities, and governments can pledge through UNEP's Web site to plant a single tree or as many as one million trees. When the tree has been planted, this can be recorded online, too.

No one who plants one of the "billion trees" and registers it online for all the world to see will ever forget how important trees are to our world. That's the power to teach that a campaign or even just a single idea can have!

In 2004, Kenyan environmentalist and human rights campaigner Professor Wangari Maathai was awarded the Nobel Peace Prize "for her contribution to sustainable development, democracy and peace." Professor Maathai is the first African woman to have won the prize.

Many of the things that scientists have helped teach us are critical to the future of our planet. When scientists discovered that the giant ice cap that covers a huge area of the Arctic Ocean at the North Pole is getting smaller each year, they studied the area year after year until they were sure that their information was correct. Then they told the rest of the world what this meant. Our world was getting warmer—the climate was changing!

The work of scientists plays a huge part in helping us learn green. They are often the first people in a long chain of educators who bring vital information about our planet to the notice of the public. Even more importantly, their work informs other scientists and people in the government and other public agencies—the people with the power to support and act on decisions that are good for the planet.

A World of Ways to Teach Green

Sometimes new information causes us to change what we think or to feel more strongly about something. We may need to listen to both sides of an issue to figure out our own opinions. Sometimes we need to dig for more information in order to understand something better. Whether it's by listening, reading, or following an example, much of what we learn comes from others who know about something and pass it along to us.

In this book, we'll take a look at some of the possibilities for teaching others about green issues, and we'll meet a whole host of people who are helping others to learn green. There are as many opportunities as there are ideas. Perhaps one will lead to the perfect green career for you!

"My greatest reward is to inspire a student, to see their eyes light up with intense excitement and a feeling that they have discovered within themselves what interests them most."

Dr. Kathleen M. Susman, college biology professor

A teacher takes her students on a nature trail. Even exploring the natural world close to the school can become an exciting experience for young children when teachers are enthusiastic about passing on their love of nature.

CHAPTER 2

TEACHING AND LEARNING GREEN IN THE CLASSROOM

Above: Young children can learn about conservation is so many ways. Growing seeds in the classroom teaches them that plants, and animals, cannot grow unless the conditions for growth are just right.

Some of the most influential people in our lives are the teachers who help and inspire us when we go to school. Whether we attend traditional or alternative schools, or if we are home schooled, those who teach us do much to shape the way we perceive and understand the world. An inspirational teacher may be someone we meet when we are in the first grade or someone who encourages us to learn something new when we are studying as an adult at night school. Even in online and distance learning, someone puts together the curriculum and responds to the students. Whatever the setting, teaching others is an awesome responsibility.

Teaching Green to the Youngest Learners

When is the best time to begin teaching a child about the environment? In her book *The Sense of Wonder*, biologist and author Rachel Carson writes about carrying her toddler nephew down to the beach on a stormy night.

Left: Making windmill models is a fun way to understand alternative methods for generating energy.

Rachel had known and loved the ocean for much of her life, but the little boy was experiencing the ocean's power for the first time. As the waves crashed on the shore, they shared the excitement, laughing together for sheer joy.

Preschool children learn about the environment by interacting with it. Their sense of wonder and curiosity means it comes naturally to them—just picture a small child and a mud puddle!

A walk around the schoolyard collecting bugs, or a visit from a nature expert with wild animals such as reptiles and amphibians, teaches children that there are millions of different species on Earth—each with its own special place in an ecosystem.

But, interaction with nature is difficult if children spend most of their time indoors. How can an urban child know about the natural world and learn to love it without experiencing it beyond the city streets?

Become a Nature Hero

That's where you, as a preschool teacher, could make a huge difference to hundreds of young children during your career. You might be teaching in a city school, surrounded by concrete, but a creative teacher can still bring nature alive. Youngsters love to pretend to be animals. Nature songs and stories are always a hit. So are art projects. Young children are fascinated with the cycles of life.

A creative teacher can get children thinking about the environment without their even realizing it! It's great fun to dress up as a rainforest leopard or make a giant mural for the classroom wall from plastic bottle tops collected by the class.

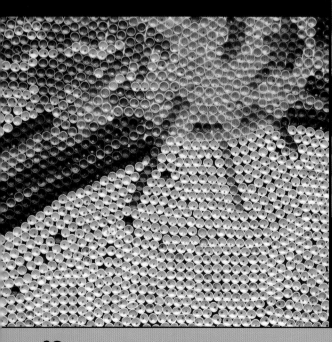

For young children, one of the most effective ways to learn is through stories. Today, many authors and illustrators tell stories featuring endangered animals and habitats.

They love growing seeds, watching caterpillars turn into butterflies, or waiting for tadpoles to turn into frogs. All these things can happen in a classroom.

A teacher can turn a walk around the school grounds or a visit to the city park into an adventure by inviting students to search for insects or differently shaped leaves.

If children do not develop a sense of respect and caring for the environment when they are very young, they may never develop that attitude at all. Think of the influence of a preschool teacher, introducing young children to the wonders of the natural world and showing them how to respect and care for it!

THE ZOO TO SCHOOL CONNECTION

The outreach program of the Saskatoon Zoo Society in Saskatchewan, Canada, offers an outreach program to the local schools. The program loans "Biofact boxes" containing biological artifacts, such as models of animal bones, for children to see and handle

The outreach program also sells owl pellets, which are little balls of indigestible food coughed up by owls. When students pick these apart carefully, they can look at the little bones inside to see what the owl ate. Best of all, the outreach program will bring a presentation about an animal right into the classroom. Yes, the animal comes, too. Topics include a hawk, a great horned owl, reptiles, ferrets, a porcupine, and more.

The Zoo Club is a lunchtime talk especially for members of a school's environment or ecology club. These programs, too, focus on one type of animal, an "animal ambassador" that comes along with the presenter. The Zoo Society interpreter explains such things as the life history of the animal and the role it plays in its native habitat.

Studying biology is just plain fun when you're getting the chance to touch a real sheep's skull and examine an owl pellet to see what a barn owl had for dinner!

Above: Children at an inner city school in the United Kingdom harvest vegetables from the school vegetable garden.

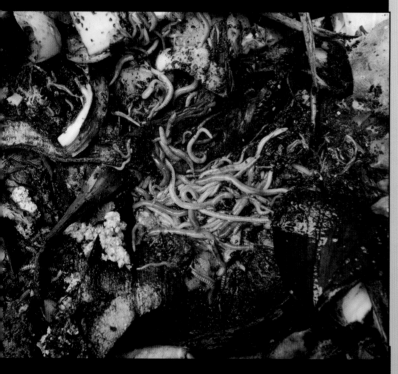

In an earthworm bin, or wormery, a community of worms eat their way through food scraps and even finely shredded paper. The worms process the food into worm casts (worm poop), or compost. This fertile, crumbly compost can be used to feed plants in a garden.

Thinking and Learning— Hands-on, Minds-on

As children develop their ability to think and reason more deeply, they move from asking "how" and "why" questions to wanting to find their own answers. A whole new world of information opens up to them as they make the transition from learning to read to reading to learn. This is a fantastic time for teachers to build on that sense of wonder.

With elementary school children, there are unlimited opportunities to teach and learn green! Hands-on real-world activities are the most fun and the most effective. Aquariums, terrariums, classroom pets—there's nothing like getting to watch and know the real thing! Nature is full of surprises. What happens if you water a pot of plain dirt from the playing field? Or put a piece of a rotting log in a jar with a lid, keep it damp, and watch it over the coming days and weeks?

Teachers also have the ability to introduce their students to many green practices such as recycling and saving energy and water. Maybe the class can build an earthworm bin where they can put their food scraps, such as apple cores and banana skins, and learn about Earth's greatest gardeners.

School gardens enable kids to learn not only about plants, but also about growing organic food—food that is grown without the use of chemical fertilizers and pesticides. What if some bugs move in and start chewing on the plants? It's an opportunity to discuss alternatives to pesticides.

Many animal conservation organizations worldwide give presentations at schools. Even very young children can become powerful advocates for animal conservation once they have come face to face with a beautiful wild animal.

BIRDS CAN BE TEACHERS, TOO!

Raptors—those magnificent birds of prey, such as eagles, hawks, falcons, and owls—are in trouble. In fact, it's a global problem. They are being injured and killed by vehicles, fences, traps, poisons, power lines, and, amazingly, people with guns.

With the help of a local veterinarian, the staff and volunteers of the Dullstroom Bird of Prey and Rehabilitation Centre in South Africa have been able to help many of the injured birds. The ideal outcome, of course, would be to be able to release the raptors back to the wild, but this can't always be done. Some of the birds will never fully recover from their injuries and would not be able to fend for themselves. Some were illegally stolen from their nests as chicks and hand raised. Now they think they are human and don't recognize their own species, so they can't go back to the wild either. The rescued birds will always have a home at the Centre, and they have become an important part of a conservation education program.

Through the Centre and through its Web site, Dullstroom is working to make people aware of the serious plight of these endangered birds. They are especially targeting school children with their message. Experts from the Centre take the raptors into schools. The students get to see the birds up close and ask the handler all sorts of questions. What an opportunity!

The Dullstroom Centre has had a good success rate with captive breeding. They are able to breed and raise birds in such a way that they do not become bonded with humans. These captive-bred birds can then be released back into the wild to help increase the numbers of a wild population that is on the brink of dying out or disappearing from a habitat where it belongs.

SPREADING THE WORD THROUGH MUSIC AND SONG: ENVIRONMENTAL EDUCATION AND YOUTH PROGRAMS COORDINATOR

My job is to oversee youth programs such as the Yukon Youth Conservation Corps. I also provide teacher support for environmental education in the schools and promote environmental education to the public.

I work with youth of all ages, but particularly those in the 11- to 20-year-old range. At the younger end of this range, kids are developing a pretty strong sense of their own values. If their personal values incorporate environmental values, then there's a good chance those values will last for life. For the older youth, I offer opportunities to put these values to practice through leadership and stewardship training and practice.

There is more than one way to get the environmental message across, and music is my choice as the most enjoyable and effective way to communicate. I use my songs throughout my presentations to schools and other groups, and I always find it rewarding to see the energy coming from the kids and to hear them singing about the environment.

CONTINUED ON PAGE 25 . . .

Remy Rodden
Environmental Education and Youth Programs
Coordinator, Musician, and Songwriter
Yukon Department of Environment
Whitehorse, Calgary, Canada

A teacher can explain that attacking one species of bug with a spray can of chemicals will also kill other types of bugs and possibly harm birds and even people when they eat the produce.

If you're a nature lover or green activist, you will be putting your passions to very good use with children of this age, because good green habits learned early are more likely to last a lifetime.

In the United States, about 2.5 million plastic bottles are used and thrown away every hour! Green learning can begin with something as simple as a preschool project to recycle bottles and end in a university research project to develop a new use for recycled plastic.

Kids with a Cause

Children can be passionate about what's not right or not fair. This is true not only of playground issues, but also about the environment, once they know what is at stake. The boundless energy of a group of nine- and ten-year-olds can propel an entire class—or even a school—to take on a green project. It's an ideal time to build a foundation of knowledge and experience involving green issues. A skillful teacher can point young people toward a lifetime of wise decisions, good stewardship, and constructive actions.

Young volunteers clear logs and other debris from the Rouge River in Redford, Michigan, during an annual river clean-up.

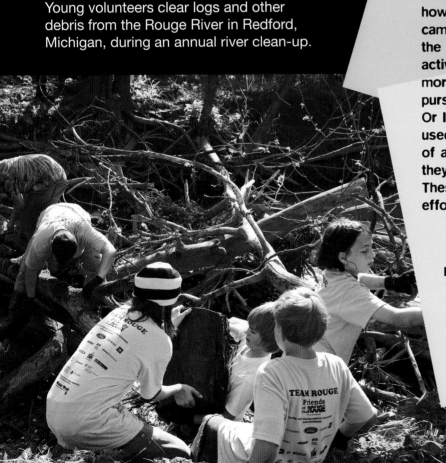

CAREER PROFILE

SPREADING THE WORD THROUGH MUSIC AND SONG: ENVIRONMENTAL EDUCATION AND YOUTH PROGRAMS COORDINATOR

. . . CONTINUED FROM PAGE 24

An important outcome of the kind of work I do is to help inspire respect and gratitude for the other-than-human world. Another is to encourage young people to learn, share, and act for the environment that supports us. Getting kids off the couch, out of the classroom, and into direct contact with living nature is vitally important and effective. These are the people who will be making decisions tomorrow. Environmental issues are not just going to go away.

I'm particularly moved when I receive feedback about the work I've done and how it impacts people. Sometimes a former camper or their parent will tell me that the experience in the wilderness and the activities we did really inspired them to do more to protect the environment or even pursue a career in the environmental field. Or I'll hear from somebody as to how they used my songs with a school class, as part of a parks interpretive program, or how they sing the songs with their grandchildren. These comments let me know that our efforts are worthwhile."

Remy Rodden
Environmental Education and Youth Programs
Coordinator, Musician, and Songwriter
Yukon Department of Environment
Whitehorse, Calgary, Canada

25

LIVING ENVIRONMENTAL HISTORY: TEACHER-RANGER-TEACHER

The Teacher-Ranger-Teacher (TRT) program connects classroom teachers with resources in a national park. During the school year, I teach 4th grade. During the summer, I'm a park ranger at an interpretive site along the Juan Bautista de Anza National Historic Trail.

The trail is part of the state history studied by California fourth graders, so I work with a lot of school groups. I love having the opportunity to make this part of California history come alive for the students.

A typical day begins at 8:00 a.m. I get the key for the Hotel (museum) that also serves as the TRT office. I go online, check for emails from headquarters, and do some research. At about 9:30 a.m. I go to the costume closet (really a whole room!) and get dressed in my trail outfit. I wear a peasant top and skirt with a shawl like some I've seen on the Web site. I'm pretending to be Gertrude Rivas, one of the people in the Anza group.

CONTINUED ON PAGE 27 . . .

Diane Barr
Teacher and Seasonal Park Interpretive Ranger
Juan Bautista de Anza National Historic Trail
San Juan Bautista, California

Environmental Action

Young adolescents are increasingly eager to participate in important decisions, especially those that affect them personally. You know this from your own experience. You might not be reading this book unless you cared about the environment and your future. You can see that you have reason to be concerned about what the world will be like in just a few years, when you are an adult. You want to learn more, you want to have meaningful discussions, and you probably want to get going on action-based projects. Who are the teachers who inspire you at this time? What do you want and need from your teachers?

Joining marches, attending political or campaign meetings, and signing online petitions are all ways in which young people can have a voice in the environmental issues that affect their lives. Here, teenagers in Detroit, Michigan, campaign against a medical waste incinerator that they say is causing pollution in their neighborhood.

26

Just think, you could be doing this for someone else a few years from now.

Teenagers equipped with solid facts and determination to make a difference can have a powerful voice in a community. Concerned young people, often from a school environmental action club, have successfully challenged businesses and government agencies over matters such as pollution and habitat destruction. Young people who want to protect the environment can look around for projects already under way or create their own. Here, again, the encouragement and expertise of a teacher or adviser can make a world of difference.

Being a green teacher doesn't mean you have to work in a school. Here, a national park ranger teaches young children about wildflowers at the Joshua Tree National Park in California.

CAREER PROFILE

LIVING ENVIRONMENTAL HISTORY: TEACHER-RANGER-TEACHER

. . . CONTINUED FROM PAGE 26

I go to the stable and set up my Anza display: a trail map, soapstone brush, drawings of the marshland, a buckeye nut, and a replica of Anza's buckskin vest. I'm there for the rest of the day, speaking to visitors about the Anza trail and explaining the objects in my display. At about 3:30 p.m. I return to the Hotel and change back into my regular uniform and head home.

I still get the chills when I tell people about this. The day after I went through the pictures and chose Gertrude Rivas, I went to a family reunion. I was reading my family history in a genealogy book when I came across the same pictures. Could someone in my family have been on the Anza expedition in 1775–1776? I read farther and found Gertrude Rivas' name. The very person I'd chosen to portray was a family ancestor!

Diane Barr
Teacher and Seasonal Park
Interpretive Ranger
Juan Bautista de Anza National
Historic Trail
San Juan Bautista, California

ONE INSPIRATIONAL TEACHER

Lisa Poole, a middle school science teacher, remembers how she first became involved in the movement to help take care of the planet:

"It was my eighth grade teacher who really got me interested in the environment and taking care of the planet. This was back in the 1970s, so he was ahead of his time. He started an environment club, and we began promoting recycling when most people didn't know what it was about. He was the first to show us nature firsthand. In class, he would show us slides of beautiful places and things of nature. The message was that these places wouldn't always be there unless we took care of them.

When he told us that a dam was planned for one of our favorite rivers, we went into action. We gathered signatures on petitions and wrote letters, and we got the issue on the ballot. In the end, the bill didn't pass, and the dam was built, but we'd made a good fight of it. In the process, we learned a lot about the power we had to speak up and be active. I still remember the excitement of hearing back from a legislator I wrote to.

We stayed involved with the club for another six or seven years after middle school, and we are still in touch. In fact, a few weeks ago, we all talked about going on another trip—37 years later!"

Lisa Poole,
middle school science teacher

Green Classes, Schools, and Clubs

Some schools offer a separate class in environmental science. Some blend it into other science classes.

Some districts offer their students the choice of attending an alternative or charter high school emphasizing environmental studies. What an opportunity for teaching and learning! In New York City, the High School of Environmental Studies combines a regular academic program with opportunities for students to get involved with green activities. While some students plant trees, others may be working with children at the city aquarium, or even be out in the neighborhoods informing voters about green issues.

High school students test samples of river water for chemicals and signs of pollution.

ECO-SCHOOLS

In the United Kingdom, the government wants every school to be a sustainable school by 2020. This means that each school will meet its own environmental needs without taking away from anyone else or from the future. At a sustainable Eco-School, green practices are a normal part of everyday school life.

Schools work toward gaining Eco-School status and can achieve a series of three awards: first Bronze, then Silver, and finally the Green Flag. The prized Green Flag award symbolizes the excellence of a school's environmental activities and its environmental success.

The students are the driving force behind a school reaching Eco-School status. They are in charge of a central eco-committee consisting of students and staff members. At the start of the program, they help assess how their school is doing. They then measure and monitor progress along the way. The program is based on nine themes: water, biodiversity, energy, global perspectives (consideration of environmental, social, and economic impacts of decisions made), healthy living, litter, school grounds, transportation, and waste. The students on the eco-committee consult with the rest of the school to decide which themes to address and how to go about doing it.

A creative design for a wind turbine with integrated climbing frame and slide. This turbine, intended to be placed on a school playground, was on display at an enviromental show in Leverkusen, Germany.

Many schools have environmental clubs actively working to promote green understanding. Western Canada High School in Calgary, Alberta, has such a club "dedicated to helping the environment, be it fundraising to help endangered species, cleaning up around our school and city, recycling, or simply educating others about environmental issues." The club sponsors school-wide events such as a Bike-In and a waste-free lunch contest. Their Web site includes upcoming environmental events and lists green stores in the Calgary area.

Many important scientific discoveries stem from university research programs. If science interests you, perhaps you could combine your love for scientific discovery with a teaching role.

University: Charting the Course for Life

Nearly every college or university offers some form of environmental studies. Some offer courses on green-related topics, perhaps within a department such as biology. Some, such as York University in Toronto, Ontario, have a separate Department of Environmental Studies. Some have designed an entire major, or emphasis, around environmental coursework. The University of Ulster in the UK includes a College of Environmental Studies. At Unity College in Maine, the entire curriculum is focused on the environment!

Colleges and universities are places to fine-tune your career goals. You have many choices among hundreds

Here, a university researcher studies the effects of raised carbon dioxide levels (due to the burning of fossil fuels) on plants. The gray tube next to the researcher connects to a device that controls carbon dioxide levels in the enclosure.

of excellent programs. It may even be that your goal is to teach at a college or university. In addition to teaching, college and university faculty carry on their own research projects. At a university, you will be choosing a life of ongoing teaching and learning.

CAREER PROFILE

A LIFE OF SCIENCE, RESEARCH, TEACHING, AND LEARNING: COLLEGE BIOLOGY PROFESSOR

I work with undergraduate students. They come with interests in science, biology, neuroscience, behavior, or medicine. I teach them in the classroom and advise them on their course selections and career choices. I'm also a research mentor, sponsoring students in my research laboratory. This gives them a chance to explore research as a possible career option.

On a typical day, I arrive at my office in a bit of a rush and check my email. I grab a few dry-erase pens, along with my laptop and course notebook, and head to class. I give a lecture using PowerPoint slides that is followed by a small group discussion. After class, I head for a meeting, deal with email, or work with one of my independent research students. Usually the day bounces from class to meetings to emails and back. During the academic year, it is a breathless, break-neck pace.

I think that my role as a biology teacher, particularly through my introductory biology course, can effectively help undergraduate students learn about the importance of "green" ways of living and interacting with the world. This knowledge will have an impact on their understanding and action throughout their lives, enabling them to make a difference wherever they are.

Dr. Kathleen M. Susman
Professor of Biology
Vassar College
Poughkeepsie, New York

CHAPTER 3

LEARNING GREEN OUTSIDE, HANDS-ON, AND UP CLOSE!

When it comes to learning about the natural world, nothing compares to experiencing as much of it as we can firsthand. For a number of reasons, a lot of people today just don't spend much time outdoors, enjoying the natural world. Too many children don't even know what they are missing. The perfect solution is environmental education: kids learning about the natural world as they are experiencing it. Field trips to zoos or time spent at camps can be fantastic learning opportunities as students experience environments different from what is most familiar to them. It also might be the perfect place for you to find a career you really love.

Above: A school field trip to the shore is a chance to explore rock pools and see marine animals such as crabs and shrimp in their natural habitat.

Right: One member of the education team at a city park stops during a nature trail to break open a poppy head and show a group of children the seeds forming inside.

Environmental Education

There are environmental education classes and experiences that are suitable for every age group and situation. Some take place right at school or at a neighborhood park.

Most state, provincial, and national parks—and even some city and county parks—have an education department. The education employees and volunteers, called docents, are trained to work with groups of young people. Docents may offer activities such as a nature hike or a close-up look at a wildlife area such as a pond. These activities may be a totally new experience for the young visitors.

MARINE MAMMAL EDUCATION

The Marine Mammal Center in California combines rescuing and rehabilitating marine mammals with educating the public about the need to care for our oceans and marine animals. Over 500 seals, sea lions, sea otters, porpoises, and other mammals are treated at the center each year. The center's research scientists study the animals and share their information with marine scientists around the world. Visitors can join talks and classes, while the center's "whale bus" visits schools with fascinating objects such as whale bones and seal skulls onboard to give schoolchildren exciting presentations about the animals found in California's waters. Everyone who works at the center—from the veterinarians to the administrators and the center's 800 volunteers—are all working toward the goal of educating the public about the conservation of marine wildlife.

Expert marine animal rescuer volunteers return a rehabilitated harbor seal to the ocean after a stay at a marine mammal rescue center. Rescuers are trained to catch seals or sea lions by having their instructor pretend to be a stranded animal. The trainee volunteers have to capture the instructor in a net and get him or her into a carrier and onto a truck—if they can!

Elementary school students enjoy a day of outdoor activities and play linked to the natural world. Many people who work in education do their job behind the scenes. They think up and create educational programs and lesson ideas for teachers to use.

Going Wild

Many organizations provide excellent resources for teaching about the environment. One of the most widely used programs in the United States is Project WILD. The program focuses on wildlife conservation and develops exciting activities for children of all ages that can be done on the school grounds or in a neighborhood park. For example, in an active tag-type game called "Oh, Deer," children discover changes in the number of deer in a region in good and lean years of food, water, and shelter. In another activity, students role-play the parts of different community members speaking up in favor of or against building a dam on a nearby river.

Project WILD creates activity sheets and information packs that teachers can use with their students. It also provides training for teachers, scout leaders, and other educators in using the material. Behind the scenes at Project WILD are many people who think up the activities, create and produce the graphics for the material, train teachers, and design and maintain Project WILD's Web site. Can you see yourself in any of those roles?

CAREER PROFILE

TRAINING TEACHERS TO TEACH GREEN: ENVIRONMENTAL PROGRAM COORDINATOR

I design and present training workshops for classroom teachers, youth leaders, and members of conservation organizations. In the workshop they learn how to use the Project WILD materials with their students.

If I am traveling to provide a training workshop, it means long hours. Two hours before it starts, I'm there setting up the training site with all the materials.

The training sessions are usually eight hours long. It means being on my feet and "mentally on" with the audience (usually between ten and 30 people) for all that time. By the time I clean up afterwards and travel home, it may be a 12- to 14-hour day. But it is so rewarding. Educator participants love the materials and are extremely excited about the possibilities. They are stimulated with new creative energy.

The best part of my job is working with educators and providing great materials to use to teach young people about the world they live in.

Bobbie Winn
Project WILD Coordinator
California Department of Fish and Game
Sacramento, California

On the left in this photograph we can see Malaysian rain forest; on the right, acres and acres of palm oil plantation. To meet growing demand, palm oil producers cut down and burn millions of acres of wild habitat to create farmland. Rain forest animals, such as orangutans, are killed or forced to move into the ever-decreasing areas of remaining forest. Over 70 percent of palm oil ends up in the food products we buy such as chocolate and cream cheese. Conservation organizations are working hard to educate consumers about this issue.

It's Just Another Bug—Isn't It?

Today, many animal species are endangered—and it's not just the famous, highly photogenic ones such as giant pandas or orangutans. Many species of birds, fish, snakes, and even insects and spiders are in danger of becoming extinct. The main reason that so many species are threatened is habitat destruction. As humans need more space to grow food and build homes, they are destroying the forests, grasslands, and water habitats that are home to the world's wildlife.

Some people might question why one species of bird is so important—or why one species of beetle becoming extinct is a problem when there are so many others. The answer to these questions is biodiversity.

Biodiversity is short for "biological diversity." It means every different type of living thing on Earth—every kind of microorganism, plant, insect, animal, and person. Biodiversity keeps our planet healthy. The existence of each living thing in an ecosystem has an impact on the other living beings in that system. Every living thing is part of a food web, eating other plants or animals or being food for something else higher up on a food chain.

If one species of animal or plant becomes extinct, it affects everything else in the chain, the ecosystem, and in the overall balance of the natural world.

That's why educating people about the importance of protecting wildlife is so crucial to the future of our planet.

Face to Face with Wildlife

When it comes to raising people's awareness of the value of wildlife and the natural environment, there's nothing like seeing the real animals face to face. One exciting way for people of all ages to learn more about wild animals and conservation is to visit a wildlife sanctuary or zoo.

CAREER PROFILE

RUNNING THE ZOOMOBILE: MANAGER OF SCHOOL PROGRAMS

I coordinate all the zoo's programs directly involved with school groups and teachers, especially the Zoomobile and field trips to the zoo. I schedule everything and often teach the programs, too. I also work on training the animals that we use for the programs. Because I work with teachers and school groups, the most important thing I have to keep in mind is to align my programs with what is being taught in class and enhance what the children are already learning.

Usually my day involves packing up animals and a program into the Zoomobile and heading out to a school to teach up to four programs. Sometimes groups come to me at the zoo. Programs include such topics as "Rain Forest—Web of Life"; "Diversity of Life"; and "Who Is Living in Your Backyard?"

Working in a zoo setting, we have the advantage of the animals. People's interest in and love for wildlife is the jumping off point from which we can deliver our conservation messages. People come to the zoo to see animals and enjoy them, but when they leave they have a new appreciation for the environment and some ideas about how they can change their habits to help wildlife. The animals truly are our ambassadors.

I like that every day is different. I get to work with animals while teaching the public about the animals and conservation issues. I have a lot of really inspiring moments every day!

Carrie Hawthorne
Manager of School Programs
Rhode Island Zoological Society
Roger Williams Park Zoo
Providence, Rhode Island

Zoo educators with a white tiger visit an elementary school to teach the students about endangered animals.

Learning to Help Animals

Today, zoos and wildlife sanctuaries are not just places to look at animals. They are places for research and discovery. They are also places for learning about animals and about how they live in their natural habitats. This wasn't always the case. Even when your parents were kids, many zoos were not designed with the comfort and happiness of the animals in mind. Animals were kept alone in empty, concrete enclosures that were not large enough for their needs. It's not that people meant to be cruel to the animals. They just didn't understand what the animals needed. People believed that if an animal had shelter, food, and water, it didn't need anything else.

Today, we know that animals need much more. We understand that animals need mental stimulation and that they have natural instincts that they need to express.

Wildlife sanctuaries around the world work to help animals and raise awareness of issues such as habitat destruction and poaching. Here (above), a keeper at a rescue center in Africa cares for a young gorilla whose mother was killed by poachers.

MEETING THE EDUCATIONAL NEEDS OF VOLUNTEERS: WILDLIFE REHABILITATION DIRECTORS

We direct a wildlife rehabilitation center for small wild animals in our area. At the center, animals that have been injured or are too young to survive on their own are treated and cared for. When they are ready, they are returned to the wild.

As directors, we are responsible for all educational and public outreach activity. We conduct research on the training needs of the wildlife rehabilitators and develop educational materials to meet those needs. The materials cover numerous topics and are useful to anyone who works in wildlife rehab, as well as those who think they might want to become involved.

We design short training sessions, seminars (one to three days), webinars (interactive online seminars), and books and other printed materials. Sometimes we direct the actual training sessions, and sometimes we serve as moderators. People from all over come to the WildAgain Web site to ask questions, find information, or download articles.

When it isn't wildlife "busy season," we research questions and topics related to wildlife. It takes a lot of time to write publications and prepare trainings.

So far, we've conducted seminars and trainings in many locations in the United States and Canada. We are now placing more priority on distance learning. This way we can keep the cost down and be available to people wherever they live.

Shirley J. and Allen M. Casey III
Co-Executive Directors
WildAgain Wildlife Rehabilitation Center, Inc.
Evergreen, Colorado

Facing page: An animal rehabilitator gently examines an injured bird. Above: Young visitors to a wildlife sanctuary get the chance to hold an orphaned baby opossum (more commonly called a possum) and an orphaned baby raccoon. Wildlife sanctuaries are a great place for the general public to learn about the wildlife in their region.

ANIMAL CONSERVATION WORK

Zoos are not just places where endangered animals can live safely. They are also places where work is taking place to try to breed animals that are endangered.

Around the world, zoos are cooperating in captive breeding programs. A zoo in Germany might only have female animals of a particular species. Therefore, a zoo in the UK will lend the German zoo its male animal for breeding. When the young are born, they might be sent to other zoos elsewhere in the world to help start more new families of that species. All this work helps preserve an endangered species.

In addition to captive breeding programs, many zoos are joining forces with organizations in the animals' original countries to return zoo-born animals to the wild to live in protected areas.

Not all scientists and conservationists agree with this approach. Many believe we should not have zoos at all. They believe that we should not keep wild animals in zoos but that we should do more to protect and preserve these animals in the wild. It's a difficult debate with good arguments on both sides. If you choose to make animal conservation your career, it will be one of the many questions you will need to consider.

A baby Madagascan aye-aye born as part of a captive breeding program at Bristol Zoo in the United Kingdom. The aye-aye is a species of lemur found only on the island of Madagascar. The aye-aye is severely endangered.

We know that animals that live naturally in groups must live with others of their kind. We also understand that animals, whether they are giant elephants or tiny ants, have complex social structures within their groups.

We know all this because of the work of research scientists who have spent years studying animals. It means we are now able to keep captive wild animals in conditions that are much kinder to them. It means that the animals are healthier and that they breed. Not everyone agrees, but most experts believe that if animals are breeding and successfully rearing their young, it is an indication that they feel safe and content.

GORILLAS GO BACK TO THE WILD

In the United Kingdom, Howletts and Port Lympne Wild Animal Parks are leading the way in animal conservation and reintroduction work. The parks were set up by a British conservationist named John Aspinall. The parks are home to many endangered animals but are most famous for their work with gorillas, like the one shown here. In fact, Howletts is home to the world's largest group of captive gorillas. Over 60 gorillas, living in family groups in large enclosures, live at the park. In conjunction with gorilla rescue and rehabilitation projects in Africa, the Aspinall Foundation is reintroducing captive-born gorillas back into the wild. The gorillas live in protected areas that are as close to their natural habitat as possible. As of May 2009, 50 gorillas from the parks have been reintroduced to the wild. The gorillas have settled happily into a wild life, and nine babies have been born to reintroduced animals.

Today, zoo animals, such as the gorillas shown here, live in family groups in large enclosures with private areas away from the public. This is healthier for the animals and gives zoo visitors the chance to learn more about how the animals live and interact in the wild.

A young visitor to the Bronx Zoo in New York City gets the chance to find out what it's like to hear like a fennec fox. Designing exhibits, like this one, that are fun yet educational are the job of the curator of exhibits.

These discoveries came just in time to make a difference in the lives of many animals and in the conservation of their habitats. As scientists were discovering more about animals and their needs, more and more habitat destruction was taking place. Today, zoos and wildlife sanctuaries are vital refuges for many endangered species. Without zoos or protected park areas, many more species would now be extinct.

Zoos as Places for Learning

Along with the conservation work going on behind the scenes at zoos to protect threatened species, zoos are what they have always been—places where people go to learn more about wild animals. They are also places where people can find jobs that will give them a chance to work with both animals and humans!

A member of a zoo's educational team shows children items on the "curiosity cart." The children get to examine items such as snake skin, a turtle's shell, and an alligator's skull!

ZOO CAREERS

Every person who works in a zoo or at a wild animal center is contributing to both the care of the animals and to the zoo or center's mission to educate people about animal conservation. Here are just some of the jobs available:

• **Keeper.** In this role you are responsible for the day-to-day care of the animals. You prepare their food, clean their enclosures, and keep records about the animals' health.

• **Conservation Zoologist.** In this role you will use your scientific knowledge of animals to advise the keepers on the best way to care for the animals. You will also conduct research projects to find out more about the animals in the zoo and sometimes overseas in their natural habitat.

• **Curator of Exhibits.** In this role you will be creating displays that give visitors information about the animals. You might create an information board with facts, photographs, and artwork, or you might be helping to create a new display that allows people to watch an army of leaf cutter ants cut up leaves and take them into their nest.

• **Development Director.** In this role you will be dreaming up and running fund-raising activities. You will also apply to the government and companies for donations of money to help the zoo carry out its work.

• **Marketing Director.** In this role you will dream up advertising campaigns to get more people to visit the zoo and get involved with fund-raising activities.

• **Membership Director.** In this role you will be responsible for getting people to join the zoo as members and frequent visitors. This ensures that the zoo has regular funds coming in. You will also run fund-raising programs such as "adopt an animal." This is a scheme in which people donate money to become the "adoptive parent" of an animal.

CAREER PROFILE

LOVING ANIMALS AND EDUCATION: MANAGER OF INTERPRETATIONS AND GRAPHICS

I love science and I like working with young adults, so I became a high school science teacher. After seven years, I decided that it was time for a career change. I have always loved zoos and wanted to work for one. That's when I became an AmeriCorps member at the zoo. (AmeriCorps is a program that offers people the chance to work with nonprofit groups and charities.)

I was responsible for maintaining the butterfly exhibit, including plant and animal care. Most of the time I was talking with visitors, pointing out things to see and answering their questions. Visitors would constantly ask how they could create a butterfly garden in their own yards. Every time I replied, I emphasized using natural methods of pest control and natural fertilizers to feed the plants. They were able to see that they could make a difference to the environment.

CONTINUED ON PAGE 45 . . .

Lynne McLain
Manager of Interpretations and Graphics
Roger Williams Park Zoo
Providence, Rhode Island

There are many ways that visitors can find out about the animals' natural habitats and the threats they face. Zoos provide information boards, guidebooks, and talks where visitors can ask the keepers questions. Working in the education department of a zoo means you might be writing and designing a Web page about the zoo's new baby leopard during the day and camping out in the park with a school group on a special zoo safari that night!

Many people dislike snakes or are afraid of them. Many snake species are endangered. Not a good mix! At zoos, reptile keepers get to introduce visitors to snakes in a safe and controlled environment and tell them all about the lives and conservation needs of these fascinating creatures.

If you have a passion for animals and want to help others learn more, zoos and wildlife sanctuaries offer many opportunities for exciting educational, animal-related careers.

CAREER PROFILE

LOVING ANIMALS AND EDUCATION: MANAGER OF INTERPRETATIONS AND GRAPHICS

. . . CONTINUED FROM PAGE 44

For my AmeriCorps project, I created an accessibility packet for the zoo. The mini-tour included close-up pictures of eight selected animals with facts and a touch component. These were made available to people with disabilities who wished to visit the zoo but who were restricted in their access to all of the animals.

One day a preteen boy came in while I was in the butterfly exhibit. When I went to speak with him, I realized he was deaf. We spent the next 30 minutes communicating without words. Before he left he gave me a hug. I realized that I'd made a difference in his day.

When the AmeriCorps position ended, I applied for a job as Manager of Interpretations and Graphics at the zoo. I got it, and that's what I'm doing now. It combines two things I love—zoos and education.

Lynne McLain
Manager of Interpretations and Graphics
Roger Williams Park Zoo
Providence, Rhode Island

Hiking, bird-watching, and collecting bugs are just three of the activities that you might introduce children to during your work as a camp counselor.

There's no microwaving or take-out in the forest! Here, a camp counselor teaches children how to light a campfire. The children have observed fire safety rules and have cleared all flammable debris from around the area of the fire to prevent a forest fire from starting.

A Week in the Wild

If a day spent in close contact with the environment is a wonderful experience, think how much fun a week can be! Outdoor education programs and camps can be a life-changing experience for those who attend.

What stands out? For some kids, especially those from urban areas, it may be the first time they've seen a snake or pond turtle, much less held one. As they look into a night sky darker than they ever could have imagined, they may be astounded at all the stars they can see. It may seem strangely silent at first, far from the city noises—and then they hear their first bullfrog. What was that? Are you sure it was an owl?

In this new and different setting, kids often surprise themselves. Who would have thought that they could hike that far or climb that mountain? Who would have believed that it could be so interesting to learn about birds while watching a nesting pair, or to figure out the path of a glacier by traces on the rocks it left behind?

LIFE AT AN ECO-FRIENDLY SUMMER CAMP

At the Kawartha Outdoor Education Centre in Ontario, Canada, children get the chance to take part in exciting activities at its summer nature camp. Traditional summer camp activities, such as canoeing, windsurfing, and arts and crafts, are combined with innovative ways to teach about the natural world and conservation. Campers get to take part in a survival game in which they role-play a wild animal. They must hide from danger, find water and food, and survive to the end of the game! A reptile zoo visits the camp to introduce the children to snakes, lizards, and crocodiles, and the children take part in hikes that have nature themes.

Life at the center is a good introduction to eco-friendly living. There are buildings made from straw bales (a very eco-friendly and renewable building material) and wind turbines producing electricity. The children can race model cars powered by solar energy and cook food using an oven powered by the Sun.

Cell phones and GPS (Global Positioning System) don't always work in the wilderness! Here, a camp counselor teaches his group how to use a compass to find which way is north.

All these wonderful nature experiences are possible thanks to the work of dedicated camp staff and counselors. Working as a counselor means you will be thinking up ways to teach the kids about the natural environment around them. You will be running the activities—getting muddy, wet, hot, and tired! You will need to make sure that everyone stays safe. You will have to keep boisterous members of the group under control and make sure that shy members join in and make friends.

Even with all the activities to enjoy and fun to be had, many camp counselors will say that introducing kids to the great outdoors and watching them respond is the very best part of the experience.

Imagine going to work each day in the great outdoors indulging your passion for all things green—and giving kids a summer they will never forget!

One of the ways in which the world learns about important green issues is through the work of conservation organizations and charities such as the Rainforest Alliance and the World Wildlife Fund. These organizations campaign to halt climate change, clean up pollution, preserve threatened habitats, and protect wild animals. If you want a career in which you can spread the word about green issues and help educate future generations, working for one of these organizations could be for you.

Every Penny Counts, Every Person Counts

Big conservation organizations spend millions of dollars every year on wildlife and environmental campaigns around the world. Before they can begin to help animals and wild habitats, or run their educational programs, they must raise the money they need for their work from membership fees and donations and through special fund-raising campaigns.

What does this mean to you in career terms? It means that conservation organizations need people to carry out work linked to fund raising.

Being employed by a conservation organization or charity might mean working the telephones and collecting donations, managing a database of members and sending out campaign newsletters, or working in the finance department collecting membership fees and managing the accounts. All this work is vital if the organization is going to be able to spread its message.

LEARNING GREEN WITH WWF

The World Wildlife Fund is the world's leading environmental organization. WWF was formed in 1961 and now works in over 90 countries around the world. Its mission is to "address global threats to people and nature such as climate change, the peril to endangered species and habitats, and the unsustainable consumption of the world's natural resources."

In the UK, WWF has launched a One Planet School scheme to link into the UK government's agenda to create Eco-Schools. The campaign will help schools reduce their impact on the planet. In another educational project WWF is working with composers to produce musicals that schools can perform. So far, WWF has produced musicals about habitat loss, rainforest destruction, and marine pollution.

A busy charity office also needs administration people to help run the business side of the office, IT (information technology) support people fixing the computers, and public relations people who talk to newspapers, answer questions from the public, and occasionally appear on TV when a green issue hits the headlines. You might not think that these jobs have much to do with learning green, but without your contribution, the organization would not be able to spread its message and carry out the many important educational programs that it runs.

Members of WWF set up 1,600 papier mache pandas in Paris in October 2008 to raise awareness that there are just 1,600 giant pandas left in the world.

Green Corps—Learning, Working, and Making a Difference

If you think that a career with an environmental organization is for you, the Green Corps program is an exciting way for you to "get your foot in the door." Green Corps is a yearlong training course in environmental activism for college graduates. Students learn in the classroom and are also linked up with environmental groups who need activists to help fight their campaigns. At the end of the course, Green Corps helps find the students jobs with environmental organizations.

Green Corps activists have been involved in many successful campaigns. In Minnesota, Green Corps organizers worked as part of a campaign that successfully helped get a new state law passed requiring that 25 percent of the state's energy come from renewable sources by the year 2020.

The educational materials produced by the Rainforest Alliance allow children in places such as North America and Europe to find out about children who live in threatened rain forests worldwide, such as these boys from the Xicrin tribe in the Amazon rain forest, Brazil.

LEARNING GREEN WITH THE RAINFOREST ALLIANCE

The Rainforest Alliance is an organization in 60 countries around the globe that works with farmers and businesses to find sustainable ways to produce timber and grow crops such as coffee and tea while protecting rainforest habitats. The Rainforest Alliance's mission is to "conserve biodiversity and ensure sustainable livelihoods by transforming land-use practices, business practices and consumer behavior."

This organization produces a wealth of educational materials that teachers and children can use to learn about rain forests, wildlife, biodiversity, and the lives of rainforest peoples. The materials include stories, coloring books, craft projects, and complete lesson plans. Schools can also help the work of small conservation groups fighting to protect rain forests worldwide by raising funds and sponsoring their own piece of rain forest under the Alliance's Adopt-A-Rainforest program.

LEARNING GREEN WITH EARTHWATCH

Earthwatch is an organization that offers members of the public the chance to work alongside leading scientific researchers in the field. Its mission is to "engage people worldwide in scientific field research and education in order to promote the understanding and action necessary for a sustainable environment."

In 2008, Earthwatch sponsored 130 research projects in over 40 countries. Earthwatch's "Teen Teams" program gives high school students the chance to join many different research projects. Students can study climate change in the Arctic, monitor whale and dolphin behavior in the Bahamas, or patrol beaches in Trinidad tagging and collecting data on leatherback turtles as they come to the island's beaches to nest. Earthwatch's "Live From the Field" program for educators gives teachers the chance to join research expeditions and connect with their students, back in the classroom, via video conferencing and blogs.

Working with the marine protection organization Oceana, Green Corps activists fought a successful campaign to stop the Royal Caribbean cruise line from dumping hundreds of thousands of gallons of sewage from its ships into the oceans. Green Corps campaigners generated media attention and a huge public protest that led to the shipping company installing pollution control technology on its ships.

If it's important to you to be right at the forefront of the movement to bring conservation issues to the public's attention, then a career with Green Corps or any other activist and charity organization might be just what you are looking for. If you want to become involved in an organization's educational programs, then a career in its educational department will put you in touch with children, teachers, and a whole host of exciting and varied projects. You can teach, learn, earn, and help others save the planet, all at once!

Earthwatch volunteers work alongside Peruvian scientists monitoring wildlife at the Lago Preto Conservation Reserve in Peru.

We can learn green in the classroom or we can learn green by visiting a zoo, wildlife sanctuary, park, or nature camp. We can also learn green by opening an environmental sciences book, clicking onto a conservation Web site, reading a magazine article, or watching a TV documentary. Books, magazines, newspapers, the Internet, television, radio, and documentary movies are all great ways to find out information about green issues.

Getting the Information onto the Page

Whether you are reading a book or using a Web site, it has taken a team of imaginative people to create that information. Writers, graphic designers, photographers, and illustrators are all important components of a creative team.

Some of the most popular stars of the *Springwatch* TV show are the barn owls. Their daily dramas are filmed using "owl cams" inside nest boxes around the UK.

SPRINGWATCH—A WILDLIFE SOAP OPERA

For several weeks each spring, BBC television in the UK broadcasts *Springwatch*, a special prime time nature show. Up to 50 hidden cameras are set up in various locations to film different birds and wild animals as they have their babies and live out their daily lives. Each night the viewers can check on each animal and bird family to see what is happening. People really get caught up in it: Did that last barn owl egg hatch? Is the small, weak baby badger going to be OK? Has the mother robin been caught by a cat?

This program has brought wildlife into people's homes in a unique way. Viewers get to follow the secret lives of birds and animals in real time. The show is a huge success and has millions of dedicated fans. It seems that many people are more interested in following the lives of animals than they are in keeping up with reality TV shows and human soap operas!

CAREER PROFILE

LEARNING THROUGH STORY AND SONG: STORYTELLER AND SONGWRITER

I tell folktales and personal stories, and I write and sing songs on various subjects including the environment. My audience is people of all ages in schools, libraries, bookstores, hospitals. . . . Occasionally I appear on radio or television.

I own a record label and have put out several CDs of my own and my friends' songs. I sell them from my Web site along with my book on storytelling.

My job has no typical days. I might wake up with an idea for a song and have time to work on it. Or, I might perform or give a workshop in the morning and later walk to the library to look for a story.

The activity I like best is writing a song. Almost anything I'm interested in can be part of my job. I've written songs about everything from earthworms to dog hair. Most of my environmental songs were written for kids aged seven to 12 years old. I think songs stick in people's minds and can remind them of a green concept when the information is useful to what they are doing. Some stories can do the same.

Nancy Schimmel
Sisters' Choice Recordings and Books
Berkeley, California

If the idea of writing or taking photographs as a way to make a living sounds exciting, maybe this could be the green career direction for you!

Writers are the people who provide the text. Maybe your skill will be writing environmental stories, poems, or songs for very young children. Maybe you will enjoy researching a subject and writing an educational book like this one. Perhaps your skill will be in writing short, catchy articles for magazines or Web sites.

It's not just books that need writers. Radio shows and TV shows are filled with words—all supplied by writers. Designers are the creative people who take all the raw material—the writer's text and the photographs or illustrations—and create the finished pages you see here using computer design programs.

Some people who work as writers or designers work for just one magazine, company, or organization, such as a conservation group (facing page). Others work freelance (above). This means they work for themselves, on their own time and out of their own homes, and market their skills to a number of different clients.

CAREER PROFILE

ASK THE BUGMAN: COLUMNIST AND AUTHOR

I write a syndicated newspaper column about bugs and pest control. ("Syndicated" means that it is published in a number of different newspapers.) I also write books and consult with the public regarding non-toxic (eco-friendly) pest control. Most of my work is in print form, but some has involved radio and television. I also maintain a Web site through which I answer questions and provide up-to-date information about pesticides and non-toxic alternatives.

In addition to my writing, I've worked as an entomologist (insect scientist) and as an integrated pest management specialist for the University of New Mexico. (Integrated pest management is effective, environmentally sensitive pest control without the use of toxic chemicals.)

A typical day for me is consulting with people about their pest problems. It's important for people to understand that pesticides aren't as safe as we are led to believe. Most of the people I work with pay attention and follow my advice. We're supposed to have control over bugs, but we aren't required to poison ourselves or pollute the planet to achieve that goal.

Richard "Bugman" Fagerlund
Veguita, New Mexico

If you love to draw or paint perhaps you will be able to use your talent to create illustrations for books or magazines. These drawings of endangered animals were created by British artist Emma Bowring.

At the beginning of this book, we talked about pollution in rivers. Words are very powerful tools, but sometimes a photograph can tell us something without the need for words.

Photographers and artists are the people who can capture our minds and imaginations with a single picture. Images can be very powerful tools for teaching.

Learning Green. Teaching Green. Your Future?

Learning about the environment can be fun and interesting. It's often active, and it gets people outdoors. Right now a lot of people are talking about it, but the most important reason to learn about the environment is that our future depends on it. Problems such as climate change, pollution, and habitat destruction will only get worse unless people— governments and the public—decide to make the necessary changes.

A career as a photographer will give you the chance to record both the beauty of our Earth and the damage that we are doing to it. Your work could be important in changing the way people live their lives.

CAREER PROFILE

RECORDING NATURE IN IMAGES AND WORDS: WILDLIFE PHOTOGRAPHER AND WRITER

My job is to record the wonders of nature, in words and images. My hope is to help people better enjoy their own time in nature, as well as to educate them about the need for sound conservation.

Ever since I was very young, I've wanted to be a writer. I found that I could combine my love of the out-of-doors with writing as a way to make a satisfying living. My photography was an outgrowth of my writing. During my college summers, I had a job outdoors. That experience, along with my biology classes, gave me a good grasp of the science of wildlife and has helped me explain nature to people. It has also helped me better understand wildlife behavior, which is a great aid in wildlife photography.

I travel a lot, but mostly within a day's drive of my home. I do not photograph or write about distant locations. I have learned that the writers and photographers who live in those places will always know more, and produce better work, than I can. The same is true in reverse. Few know "my" neck of the woods as well as I do, so I can produce better results by staying closer to home.

I consider my role as an educator to be very important. My work has always had either a clear tone or an undercurrent expressing an environmental and conservation ethic. I know it has inspired some people, and that is a great feeling.

Michael Furtman
Freelance photographer
Duluth, Minnesota

Wise decisions and good stewardship aren't going to happen unless people know the facts and understand how everything in the natural world is designed to work together. Everyone needs to realize the consequences if the environment isn't respected and cared for. A plant or animal that is extinct is gone forever, but we can turn around many of the problems we have caused and help the environment heal.

Right now, you spend a lot of your time learning, but you could also be teaching. What can you do to help others learn green right now?

Soon, you will start to think about the future and what kind of career you might want to have. It's an important choice to make. Perhaps it will involve helping others learn green.

It's time to do everything we can to help our planet, whether that's walking instead of driving, taking a shower to save water instead of a bath, or recycling. Today, kids are eager to spread the message—the future is green!

START YOUR GREEN FUTURE NOW...

t's exciting to have plans and dreams for the future. It's also exciting to try new things. While you wait for school to be over, here are some fun projects to help you find out what you enjoy doing and to whet your appetite for your future career.

GET INVOLVED WITH AN ENVIRONMENTAL ACTION SCHOOL CLUB

If your school has an environmental action club, join it and get into the action. If there isn't such a club, get together with some of your friends and a supportive teacher and start one. This could be an ideal opportunity to learn about and practice ways of both modeling green living and teaching others about important environmental issues. Look on the Internet to see what other environment clubs are doing, such as the one at Western Canada High School.

PRACTICE

Others around you may not know that much about the environment. Practice sharing your concerns in ways that will help them understand. It's not always easy to share information in such a way that those who hear you end up agreeing with you, but it's never too soon to be developing and practicing good communication skills. These will be especially important if you choose a career that involves interaction with the public.

BE SMART, BE SAFE!

Please get permission from the adult who cares for you before making trips to new places or volunteering in your free time. Always let him or her know where you are going and who you are meeting.

TEACH YOUNGER CHILDREN

Do you like working with younger kids? Consider the possibility of starting a neighborhood "green" club, or working with an existing club through your community. Another possibility might be assisting with an after-school club at a local elementary school. You could start with something as basic as a neighborhood cleanup and teaching the kids how to recycle the trash they bring in. Perhaps there's a neighborhood, school, or community project just waiting for the high energy of a bunch of kids led by a knowledgeable and committed leader—you!

JOIN A CONSERVATION ORGANIZATION

There are many environmental and wildlife conservation organizations around the world that welcome students. Different organizations have different objectives. Some work on global issues; others concentrate on a particular region of the world or a certain endangered species. Look for one that focuses on a cause that is especially important to you. By joining and being active, you can support important work and gain valuable experience in ongoing conservation efforts. You may even find opportunities to participate in conservation fieldwork that would be excellent experience and perhaps even lead to a future career.

READ, LISTEN, LEARN

The people whose careers were profiled in this book had some wise advice for those who would like to pursue similar careers in learning green. First: Read, read, read! In addition to increasing your own knowledge, you never know when something you've read will be useful. Second: Keep learning a variety of practical skills. Talk to people who are working in a field that interests you and ask specifically what skills you'll need to know. Whatever you do, you can be sure that technology will play an important part, too. Third, get as much experience as you can. If it's a career that uses volunteers, take advantage of that opportunity to find out what the career really involves. If it's not a career that makes use of volunteers, ask if you can "shadow" someone, observing their daily work to learn more about what they do. With just about any job you are interested in, actually doing it or watching closely while someone else does it will help you decide if it is the right job for you. Fourth, ask questions. Most people are happy to talk about the work they do when asked by someone who is considering following a similar career path.

activist A person with a strong belief in a cause who participates in direct action to bring about change

biodiversity Biological diversity—the numbers of different species of living things

biological artifacts Human-made models representing objects such as animal bones or teeth

carbon footprint The way in which we measure how much carbon dioxide, or CO_2, a person, a building, or a business is responsible for. For example, each time people go for a ride in a car or use electricity, their activities produce CO_2. Their carbon footprint is the amount of CO_2 they are responsible for

climate change A gradual warming of Earth's climate. It is caused by the burning of fossil fuels that give off greenhouse gases and trap too much of the Sun's heat in the Earth's atmosphere

database An organized collection of information such as records stored in a computer system

docent Volunteer trained in guiding visitors, giving explanations, and answering questions at sites such as museums, historic sites, and aquariums

entomologist A scientist who specializes in the study of insects

food chain A feeding relationship of certain organisms in an ecosystem. For example, a caterpillar eats the leaves on a plant; a robin eats the caterpillar; a hawk eats the robin. Food chains are strands of an overall food web including all eating relationships within that ecosystem

fossil fuels Fuels, such as oil, coal, and gas, that formed over the course of millions of years from the decaying remains of plants and animals

fungi A group of living organisms including yeast, molds, toadstools, and mushrooms

global warming A gradual warming of Earth's climate (see: climate change)

greenhouse effect The rise in Earth's temperature caused by certain gases in the atmosphere that trap energy from the Sun. These gases are causing the Sun's heat to become trapped in Earth's atmosphere—just as the glass of a greenhouse traps heat— and cause climate change

greenhouse gases Gases in Earth's atmosphere including carbon dioxide, water vapor, nitrous oxide, ozone, and methane. A certain level of these gases occurs naturally, but burning fossil fuels adds significantly to the amount in the atmosphere

integrated pest management Effective, environmentally sensitive approach to pest management by the most economic means and with the least possible damage to people, property, and the environment

multimedia Different forms of technology working together to communicate information

nonprofit Not conducted or maintained for the purpose of making money. A nonprofit organization is usually established for a specific purpose (such as protecting endangered wildlife or rescuing mammals). The expenses of running the organization are met by fundraising and contributions

nonrenewable resources Natural resources that cannot be produced, regenerated, re-grown, or reused quickly enough to balance the rate at which they are being consumed

species A group of organisms with certain shared characteristics different from other organisms. Only members of the same species can reproduce

stewardship Careful and responsible management of something entrusted to one's care

sustainable Capable of being continued or used with little or no long-term effect on the environment

syndicated Managed by an agency and published in multiple newspapers or magazines

FURTHER INFORMATION

www.cbe.ab.ca/new/enmax.asp
See what some Canadian schools are doing to raise environmental awareness.

www.greenforall.org/
Go to "Green For All" to find out about Green Collar Careers.

www.greenforall.org/resources/green-jobs-guidebook
Download this *Green Jobs Guidebook*, which profiles over 200 green jobs with details about the experience or qualifications needed.

www.climatecrisis.net/thescience/
Active Web site of information built around the film/DVD *An Inconvenient Truth*. Includes educational support, science background about climate change, ways to take action, and more.

www.cmnonline.org/Environment.htm
The Children's Music Network offers an environmental page of music resources to teach children about environmental issues.

www.eco.ca/Portal/public_Educator.aspx
ECO Canada maintains a Web site for education-related green career possibilities.

www.earthwatch.org/
Read more about Earthwatch's mission to bring together volunteers and scientists on research programs that will help to save our planet.

www.wwf.org/
Read more about the research, educational, and fund-raising progams of the World Wildlife Fund.

www.nmfs.noaa.gov/pr/acoustics/
Background information on Volker Deecke's work with marine mammal communication.

www.michaelfurtman.com
Samples of Michael Furtman's photography, along with books and articles about the natural world.

www.rainforest-alliance.org/
Find out more about the Alliance's work to protect rain forests worldwide and their work to educate the public about the importance of these wild habitats.

www.eco-schools.org.uk/
Learn more about Eco-Schools.

ABOUT THE AUTHOR

Suzy Gazlay is an award-winning teacher and writer of children's nonfiction books. Her experience includes developing educational curriculum, and she frequently serves as a content and curriculum consultant. She enjoys music, especially singing, and has written a collection of songs for children highlighting bits of science information.

Printed in the USA—CG